KEEP PORTLAND
WEIRD COOKBOOK

Funky Food for
The Hungry Hipster

By Tim Murphy

Copyright 2017
Shamrock Arrow Media

KEEP PORTLAND WEIRD COOKBOOK

Funky Food for
The Hungry Hipster

TABLE OF CONTENTS

RECIPES

APPLE CIDER BRUSSELS SPROUTS

2 pounds of Brussels sprouts
1 cup of apple cider
2 slices of bacon, cooked and crumbled
1 tablespoon of avocado oil
1 teaspoon of salt
½ teaspoon of garlic powder
¼ teaspoon of pepper

Trim the Brussels sprouts and cut them in half. In a bowl, combine Brussels sprouts, oil salt, pepper, garlic powder and mix thoroughly. Place the sprouts on a baking sheet cut side down. Bake at 400 degrees for 30 minutes. Pour apple cider in a skillet and cook over medium heat for 10 minutes. Do not let it boil but reduce it down to a light syrup. Add roasted sprouts and crumbled bacon to the skillet and stir until sprouts are coated.

BANANA PUDDING

5-ounce package of instant vanilla pudding
  mix
14 ounces of sweetened condensed milk
16 ounces of vanilla wafers
12 bananas, sliced
2 cups of cold milk
1 tablespoon of vanilla extract
Whipped cream or Cool Whip

In a large mixing bowl, combine pudding mix and cold milk and beat for 2 minutes. Stir in the sweetened condensed milk until smooth. Stir in vanilla and fold in whipped topping. In a large glass trifle bowl, make 6 layers of wafers, bananas, pudding, wafers, bananas and pudding. Chill for at least 2 hours in the refrigerator.

BANANGO SMOOTHIE

6 ounces of almond milk
½ banana, frozen
½ cup of mango, frozen
1 scoop of vanilla whey protein

Put all ingredients in a blender and process until smooth.

BLUE CHEESE BUCKWHEAT CORNBREAD

1¼ cups of milk
1 cup of buckwheat flour
1 cup of blue cheese, crumbled
2 eggs
2 scallions, thinly sliced
½ stick of butter, melted
½ cup cornmeal
¼ cup granulated sugar
2½ teaspoons of baking powder
½ teaspoon salt

Line a 12-cup muffin tin with paper liners or lightly grease the cups. In a large bowl, whisk together buckwheat flour, cornmeal, sugar, baking powder and salt. In a second bowl, whisk together milk, butter and eggs. Pour wet ingredients into dry ingredients; stir until just combined. Fold in blue cheese and sliced scallions. Divide batter among prepared muffin cups. Bake at 400 degrees for 20 minutes or until a toothpick tests clean inserted in the center of a muffin. Remove from oven and let cool.

BLUEBERRY, QUINOA & KALE SALAD

2 cups of cooked quinoa
1½ cups of shredded kale
1 cup of fresh blueberries (not frozen)
¾ cup of feta cheese, crumbled
½ cup of almond slivers
3 tablespoons of lemon juice, fresh squeezed
2 tablespoons of olive oil
Salt and pepper to taste

In a bowl thoroughly mix quinoa, kale, blueberries, feta cheese and almond slivers. Toss with olive oil and lemon juice until completely coated. Season the salad with salt and pepper to taste.

BUFFALO CHICKEN MEATBALLS

1 pound of lean chicken, ground
¾ cup of Panko breadcrumbs
' ¾ cup of Louisiana hot sauce
¼ cup of celery, diced fine
1 egg white

In a bowl, mix breadcrumbs, celery, egg white and half of the hot sauce. Add the chicken and mix thoroughly but delicately. Form into 20 to 24 balls. Place on a greased rack on top of a baking sheet. Bake at 400 degrees for 20 to 25 minutes. Once cooked toss the meatballs with remaining hot sauce. Have some ranch dressing on the side for dipping.

CAJUN FOOD TRUCK FRIES

4 russet potatoes, cut into strips
¼ cup + 2 tablespoons of Parmesan cheese
¼ cup of parsley, finely chopped
2 tablespoons of oil
2 teaspoons of Creole seasoning
   (Try Zatarain's Big & Zesty)

Wash, peel and slice potatoes into strips. Soak in water than dry thoroughly. Mix the potatoes with oil and Creole seasoning and spread on a baking sheet. Make sure potatoes are well coated. Bake at 400 degrees for 20 minutes. Flip the potatoes after 10 minutes to brown thoroughly. After cooking, coat potatoes with Parmesan cheese and parsley

CARROT & FENNEL SOUP

1 pound of carrots, sliced into thin strips
4 cups of vegetable broth
1 bulb of fennel
½ cup of onion, diced
2 teaspoons of ginger, ground
1 teaspoon of coriander, ground
½ teaspoon of salt
¼ teaspoon of pepper
Olive oil

Toss carrots with olive oil. Put in a pan and roast at 400 degrees for 20 minutes. Heat 1 tablespoon of olive oil in a pot over medium. Trim fronds from fennel. Slice fennel bulb thinly. Add fennel and onion to the pot and stir to coat with oil. Cook, stirring occasionally, until it softens and starts to caramelize. Stir in ginger, coriander, salt, and pepper. Once the carrots have roasted, add them to the pot and pour in the vegetable broth. Bring everything to a boil then reduce to a simmer for 10 minutes. In a blender or food processor, puree soup until smooth.

CHEESE STRAWS

1 cup of flour
½ cup of cheddar cheese, grated or shredded
½ teaspoon of salt
1/3 cup of shortening
3 tablespoons of water

Mix flour salt, cheese and shortening. Add water. Roll very thin and cut into strips. Put on a greased cookie sheet and bake at 425 degrees for 10 minutes.

CHICKEN FRIED BACON

Thick cut bacon
Buttermilk
Flour
Salt
Pepper
Oil

Dip the bacon slices in buttermilk then dredge slices in flour. Salt and pepper the slices to taste. Heat the oil in a skillet and fry the bacon until golden brown. This bacon also makes an amazing BLT.

CHICKEN WAFFLE POPS

3 pounds of boneless chicken breasts
3 eggs
3 tablespoons of milk
4 cups of corn flakes, crushed
Salt and pepper to taste
Wooden skewers
 Waffle Batter:
4 cups of Bisquick
2½ cups of milk
2 tablespoons of vegetable oil
2 eggs

Cut chicken breasts in half lengthwise then into thin slices. Whisk together eggs, milk, salt and pepper in a bowl until thoroughly mixed. Drop in chicken pieces. Place the crushed corn flakes in a shallow bowl. Dredge the chicken in corn flakes to coat and place them on a lined baking sheet. Bake chicken for about 15 minutes or until cooked through. Place a wooden skewer into each piece of chicken. Preheat waffle iron. Brush iron lightly with oil or nonstick spray. Whisk Bisquick, milk, oil and eggs until thoroughly combined. Dip chicken into waffle batter then place on the waffle iron with the skewer sticking out of iron. Cook in batches. Serve with sauce of syrup of your choice.

CHICKPEA SALAD SANDWICH

15 ounces of canned chickpeas, rinsed and
    drained
¼ cup of roasted sunflower seeds, unsalted
3 tablespoons of mayonnaise or Tahini
½ teaspoon of Dijon or spicy mustard
1 tablespoon of maple syrup or honey
¼ cup of red onion, diced
2 tablespoons of fresh dill, finely chopped
Salt and pepper to taste
4 pieces of dense bread, toasted
Slices of avocado, onion, tomato and lettuce

Place chickpeas in a bowl and lightly mash with a fork. Add sunflower seeds, mayo, mustard, maple syrup, red onion, dill, salt and pepper and mix thoroughly. Adjust seasonings as needed. Toast the bread and prepare sandwich toppings. Place a scoop of the salad onto two of the pieces of bread, add desired toppings and top with other two slices of bread. Share the second sandwich with a friend.

CHILI LIME TROUT

2 whole trout, cleaned
¾ teaspoon of salt
¾ teaspoon of pepper
1 tablespoon of vegetable oil
1 tablespoon of lime juice, fresh
2 limes
14 thin slices ginger root
3 cloves of garlic, sliced thin
20 sprigs fresh coriander
2 red finger chili peppers, cut in half

Sprinkle the insides of the fish with 1/2 teaspoon each of salt and pepper. Place in shallow greased roasting pan. Rub fish all over with oil and lime juice. Slice 1 lime. Stuff slices, ginger, coriander and red chili peppers into the fish cavities. Sprinkle outsides with remaining salt and pepper. Bake fish at 425 degrees for about 25 minutes or until flesh flakes easily when tested with fork. Transfer fish and any juices to a platter. Peel back skin; lift each filet off bones. Quarter remaining lime; serve with fish.

CHOCOLATE BACON

12 slices of thick-cut bacon
12 wooden skewers
1 cup of semi-sweet chocolate chips
1 tablespoon of shortening

Thread each piece of bacon on to a skewer. Place baking rack on a cookie sheet and place bacon skewers on the rack. Bake at 400 degrees for 20 to 25 minutes until bacon is crisp. Remove from oven and let cool. Put chocolate and shortening in a microwave-safe bowl. Heat for 20 seconds spurts, stirring after each interval until mixture is completely smooth. Paint each bacon strip with chocolate and place on wax paper. Cool in the refrigerator for at least 1 hour.

CLAM BURGERS

1 pint of razor clam necks, uncooked
2 eggs
1 teaspoon of parsley flakes
2½ teaspoons of onion flakes
Tabasco or hot sauce to taste
2 teaspoons of Worcestershire sauce
¼ teaspoon of pepper
1 teaspoon of biscuit mix
3 saltine crackers
Butter
Hamburger buns

Grind the clams. Beat the eggs and add parsley flakes, dried onion flakes, Tabasco, Worcestershire sauce, pepper and biscuit mix. Crumble saltine crackers and add all of these ingredients to ground, mixed clams and mix well. Form small patties and fry in ½ to 1 inch of oil in a pan. Brown the patties well on both sides. Serve on hamburger buns.

COCONUT CHAI TEA

1 cup of boiling water
1 Chai tea bag
½ cup of coconut milk
Honey to taste
Cinnamon

Boil the water and pour over the tea bag in a mug. Let steep for 5 minutes and remove the tea bag. Pour the coconut milk into a pan and heat until it begins to steam. Froth the milk with a whisk or hand blender. Pour the frothed coconut milk over the tea and top with a sprinkle of cinnamon.

COLA CAKE

2 cups of flour
2 cups of sugar
1½ cups of miniature marshmallows
½ cup of shortening
½ cup of butter
3 tablespoons of cocoa powder
1 cup of cola
½ cup of buttermilk
1 teaspoon of baking soda
2 eggs, well beaten

In a bowl, sift together flour and sugar and mix with marshmallows and set aside. In a pan combine shortening, butter, cocoa powder and cola. Heat slowly until ingredients melt. Remove from heat and pour over the flour mixture. Stir in buttermilk, soda and eggs. Continue to stir until you have a consistent batter. Pour batter into a greased and floured baking pan. Bake the cake at 350 degrees for 45 minutes or until it tests done with a toothpick. Frost with vanilla icing or whipped cream. What cola should you choose? Pepsi is sweeter but Coke has undertones of cinnamon. Cherry cola works too if you use the right brand.

COLD BREW COFFEE

2 cups of premium coffee, coarsely ground
4 cups of water, spring or filtered

Put the coarsely ground coffee in a pitcher with the water and stir. Put a lid on the pitcher and let steep in a refrigerator for 12 to 24 hours. Slowly strain coffee through a filter to remove the grounds. This makes a very strong, concentrated coffee. Pour over ice and mix milk, cream, sugar or flavoring of choice.

CREAMY BACON SPAGHETTI

8 ounces of spaghetti, uncooked
6 strips of bacon
1 clove of garlic, minced
½ cup of whipping cream
1 cup of Parmesan cheese, grated
Fresh parsley,
Salt & pepper to taste

In a pot of salted water, cook spaghetti according to directions. Chop bacon into small pieces and cook in a skillet until crispy. Remove the skillet from the heat and mince the garlic into the skillet and stir. Once the spaghetti is cooked, drain it and return it to the pot. Return the pot to medium heat and add in the Parmesan and cream. Add the bacon to the pot, being careful to leave most of the bacon fat in the skillet. Mix the spaghetti with the cream, cheese, and bacon, and then serve after sprinkling with chopped parsley and salt and pepper to taste.

CREAMY MATCHA GREEN SMOOTHIE

> 1 cup of coconut milk
> 1 mango
> 2 bananas, frozen
> 5 ounces of baby spinach
> 2 teaspoons of Matcha Green Tea powder

In a blender, mix coconut milk, Matcha Green Tea powder and spinach and mix thoroughly. Add the mango and bananas and blend until smooth and creamy.

CRICKETS, PEAS & CABBAGE

½ cup of crickets
1 cup of snap peas, chopped
1 cup of red cabbage, chopped
1 clove of garlic, crushed
1 tablespoon of oil
Pinch of salt

Heat oil in a skillet. Stir-fry the peas, cabbage and crickets for 1 to 2 minutes. Add in garlic and continue cooking until the dish reaches your desired level of doneness. Sprinkle with salt.

CUBAN SANDWICH

1 loaf of Cuban bread
1 pound of ham
   (sweet cured ham or bolo ham works best)
1 pound of Cuban pork (or roast pork)
½ pound of Swiss cheese
16 slices of dill pickle
Butter

His recipe makes 4 sandwiches. Heat a griddle or large fry pan to medium hot. Cut bread into 8-inch sections then slice these in half. Spread butter inside on both halves. Layer ingredients as follows: pickles, roast pork, ham and cheese. Spread a little butter on the hot griddle or fry pan and place the sandwich on the hot surface. Use a foil-wrapped brick to flatten the sandwich. Squeeze it down to half or a third or its original size. Grill the sandwiches for two to three minutes then flip them over to toast the other side. Once the cheese is melted and the bread is golden brown on both sides, the sandwiches are done.

DAIRY FREE FUDGESICLES

2 avocadoes, skinned with pit removed
¾ cup + 1 tablespoon of cocoa powder
1/3 cup of nondairy milk (soy, almond, etc.)
¼ cup of Agave nectar
2 tablespoons of vanilla extract
¼ teaspoon of salt

Put all of the ingredients into a food processor or blender and process until smooth. Pour the mixture into Popsicle form. Place the form into a freezer for at least 12 hours. To remove a Fudgesicles from the form, briefly run the form under hot water until it releases from the form.

DEATH IN THE AFTERNOON

Absinthe
Champagne

Mix 1 part Absinthe to 6 parts Champagne. You can mix it stronger, but that's up to you. If you're drinking *real* Absinthe, tread carefully especially if you are a first-timer.

DEEP FRIED BACON & P.B. BITES

Peanut Butter
Bacon strips, cut in half
Flour
1 - 2 Eggs, beaten
Panko crumbs
Oil

Spoon peanut butter into plastic or silicon ice cube trays and freeze. After freezing, remove the peanut butter cubes and coat them with flour. Dip them in the egg wash and roll in Panko crumbs. Wrap the bacon around the bites so all six sides of the cubes are covered. Lower the bites into a deep fryer at 375 degrees for 60 to 90 seconds. Experiment with the frying time so the liquid peanut butter doesn't turn into molten lava!

DEEP FRIED MAC & CHEESE

3 cups of cooked macaroni & cheese
1½ cups of Panko crumbs
2 eggs, beaten
2 to 3 cups of vegetable oil

Place macaroni and cheese into the refrigerator for 4 hours or until firm. Heat vegetable oil in a large stockpot or Dutch oven over medium high heat. Using a melon baller or ice cream scoop, roll macaroni and cheese into 1½-inch balls. Dip balls one at a time into eggs, then dredge in Panko, pressing into the Panko coat to thoroughly coat. Add balls to the Dutch oven and cook until golden brown and crispy. That takes 3 to 4 minutes. Transfer to a paper towel-lined plate.

DRY ROASTED GRASSHOPPERS

1 cup of grasshoppers (dead)
Olive oil
Salt
Pepper
Seasoning of choice (optional)

Spread grasshoppers on a baking sheet and bake at 350 degrees for 10 minutes. Take them out of the oven and toss with olive oil. Sprinkle with salt and pepper to taste. You can also season with garlic salt, onion salt, red pepper flakes or seasoning of choice.

EDAMAME DIP

4 cups of water
2 cups of shelled Edamame, frozen
¼ cup of extra virgin olive oil
2 tablespoons of fresh lemon juice
1 tablespoon of soy sauce
1 tablespoon of Hoisin sauce
1½ teaspoons of grated ginger
1 clove of garlic, chopped
¼ teaspoon of kosher salt

Put the Edamame in a pan and add 4 cups water. Bring to a boil and cook, stirring occasionally for 6 to 7 minutes until very tender. Drain and rinse the Edamame under cold water until the beans are room temperature. Put the Edamame in a blender or food processor and pulse a few times. Mix in the lemon juice, soy sauce, Hoisin, ginger, garlic and salt. Process the ingredients for 1 minute, until relatively smooth. With the motor running, slowly pour in the olive oil and continue processing for another minute until the dip becomes uniform and slightly fluffy.

FISH SAUCE CHICKEN WINGS

3 pounds of chicken wing parts
1 cup of cornstarch
½ cup of fish sauce
½ cup of fine sugar
4 cloves of garlic, 2 crushed and 2 minced
2 tablespoon of oil
1 tablespoon of cilantro, chopped fine
1 tablespoon of mint, chopped
Oil for frying

In a bowl whisk the fish sauce, sugar and crushed garlic together thoroughly. Add the wings and toss to coat. Refrigerate for 3 hours, mixing the wings a few times. Heat 2 tablespoons of oil in a skillet. Stir in minced garlic and cook over moderate heat for 3 minutes or until golden brown. Drain on paper towels. In a large pot, heat 2 inches of oil to 350 degrees. Pat the wings dry on paper towels; reserve the marinade. Put the cornstarch in a shallow bowl, add the wings and toss to coat. Fry the wings in batches until golden and cooked through, about 10 minutes. Drain on paper towels and transfer to a bowl. In a saucepan, simmer the marinade over moderately high heat until syrupy, 5 minutes. Strain over the wings and toss. Top with the cilantro, mint and fried garlic and serve.

GOAT CHEESE TRUFFLES

8 ounces of plain goat cheese
4 ounces of softened cream cheese
¼ cup of pecans, chopped
¼ cup of dried cranberries, chopped
¼ cup of mint, parsley or basil, minced

In a bowl, combine the cheeses thoroughly until smooth and creamy. Refrigerate for 30 minutes. In a second bowl, mix the pecans, cranberries and mint (basil or parsley). Scoop 1 tablespoon of the cheese mixture and make a ball. Drop the ball into the bowl with the coating ingredients and gently roll the cheese ball until completely coated with the mixture. Place truffles on wax paper and refrigerate until ready to serve.

GREEK FRAPPE ICED COFFEE

2 tablespoons of evaporated milk
2 teaspoons of instant coffee
2 teaspoons of sugar
Cold water
Ice cubes

Put the coffee, sugar and 2 tablespoons of cold water in a jar, hand mixer or blender. Cover and shake well or blend for 20 to 30 seconds to produce a thick, light-brown foam. Place a few ice cubes in a tall glass. Slowly pour the coffee foam into the glass. Fill the glass with water, adding evaporated milk to taste. Serve the frappe immediately.

GREEN JUICE SMOOTHIE

2 cups of spinach
2 cups of coconut or almond milk
2 cups of diced fruit, bananas, orange, apple,
   pear or peach
1 cup of frozen berries

Blend the spinach and coconut/almond milk
together in a blender or food processor. Add the
frozen fruit to the mixture and process until smooth.

GRILLED CHEESE & PEAR SANDWICH

Sour Dough Bread
Butter
Tillamook brand sharp Cheddar, sliced
Tillamook brand Havarti, sliced
Mayonnaise
Creamy Horse Radish Sauce
Bacon Bits
French's French Fried Onions
Pear Jam or Preserves

For each sandwich butter one side of each slice of bread. On the other, spread one with a mixture of mayonnaise and horseradish sauce and one with the pear jam. Then between the 2 slices, add a slice of each cheese, bacon bits and French fried onions. Close and fry in pan until golden brown and cheese has melted.

KALE & APPLE SALAD

1 large bunch of kale
1 Honey crisp apple, diced large
1 bulb of fennel, sluiced thin
¼ cup of goat cheese, crumbled
¼ cup of dried cranberries, chopped
¼ cup of pecans, chopped
Sea salt

Cut and remove the tough ribs from the kale and discard. Chop the kale leaves into small, bite-sized pieces and put in a large salad bowl. Sprinkle a small pinch of sea salt over the kale and massage the leaves with your hands. Add apple, fennel, goat cheese and cranberries to the kale and toss. Drizzle dressing of choice over the salad in the bowl and toss again.

KALE CHIPS

½ bunch of kale leaves
½ tablespoon of extra virgin olive oil
1½ tablespoons of nutritional yeast
1 teaspoon of garlic powder
¾ teaspoon of chili powder
½ teaspoon of onion powder
½ teaspoon of smoked paprika
¼ teaspoon of fine grain sea salt

Line a baking sheet with parchment paper. Remove leaves from the stems of the kale and tear it into large pieces. Wash and thoroughly dry the kale. Put kale leaves in a large bowl. Coat leaves with oil until thoroughly coated. Combine all of the seasonings, sprinkle on the kale and toss. Spread the kale onto the baking sheet into a single layer. Bake at 300 degrees for 10 minutes, rotate the pan, and bake for another 12-15 minutes until the kale begins to firm up. Let the kale cool on the sheet for 3 minutes.

MUSHROOM PIE

17 ounces of frozen puff pasty, thawed
10 ounces of fresh mushrooms, sliced
1 cup of Swiss cheese, shredded
¾ cup of heavy whipping cream
1 onion, diced
1 egg, beaten
4 slices of bacon, chopped
1 tablespoon of olive oil
1 teaspoon of fresh dill, chopped
Salt and pepper to taste

Heat the olive oil in a skillet over medium-high heat. Add mushrooms, onion and bacon. Cook and stir for 5 minutes or until vegetables are tender. Reduce the heat to medium and add the cream and dill. Cook and stir for about 10 more minutes. Remove from the heat and stir in the cheese. Place one sheet of puff pastry on a well oiled baking sheet or pie plate. Pour the mushroom filling over the top. Cover with the other sheet, and press the edges together to seal. Make some holes in the top with a fork. Brush the top with beaten egg. Bake at 350 degrees for 40 minutes or until golden brown.

NORTHWEST HOT DOGS

¼ cup of butter
1 sweet onion thinly sliced
4 ounces of cream cheese
4 salmon hot dogs
4 hot dog buns
Spicy brown mustard
Sauerkraut

Slowly melt butter in a skillet over medium heat. Add onions, and cook for 15 minutes or until the onions have softened and turned brown. Warm cream cheese over low heat in a small pan until very soft. Grill hot dogs until fully cooked. Lightly toast hot dog buns on both sides. Spread warm cream cheese on toasted hot dog bun, add hot dog, top with onions, mustard and sauerkraut.

NUTTY IRISHMAN

6 ounces of fresh, hot coffee
1 ounce of Bailey's Irish Crème
1 ounce of Frangelico

Mix and enjoy. If you have more than 2, call Uber for a ride home.

OATMEAL PANCAKES

1 cup of quick-cooking oats
1 cup of buttermilk
¼ cup of all-purpose flour
1 egg
2 tablespoons of butter, melted
1 tablespoon of sugar
½ teaspoon of baking powder
½ teaspoon of baking soda
¼ teaspoon of cinnamon
Pinch of salt
Cooking spray

In a bowl, thoroughly whisk together flour, oats, sugar, baking powder, baking soda, cinnamon and salt. In a second bowl combine buttermilk, butter and egg. Add the wet mixture to the flour mixture, stirring just until moist. Heat a nonstick griddle or skillet over medium heat. Coat skillet with cooking spray. Spoon small ladles of batter per onto the griddle or pan. Turn pancakes over when tops are covered with bubbles; cook until bottoms are lightly browned.

OREGON COAST CRAB SALAD BURGER

2 cups of cooked Dungeness crab, shredded
1 cup of sharp cheddar cheese, shredded fine
1 - 1½ cups of mayonnaise or Miracle Whip
1 teaspoon of lemon juice
Garlic powder to taste
6 to 8 hamburger buns

Mix all ingredients. Scoop mixture onto hamburger buns and bake in the oven at 350 degrees until the cheese is bubbly. Works in a toaster oven and broiler too.

PUMPKIN SMOOTHIE

1 cup of non-unsweetened almond milk
½ cup of canned pumpkin
½ banana
½ teaspoon of maple syrup
½ teaspoon of vanilla extract
¼ teaspoon of ground cinnamon
⅛ teaspoon ground ginger
Pinch of ground nutmeg
Pinch of ground cloves
Pinch of all spice

Drop all of the ingredients into a blender and process until smooth. If you like, drop in some ice cubes while blending.

PUMPKIN SPICE GRANOLA

2½ cups of rolled oats
¾ cup of dried cranberries
1/3 cup toasted pumpkin seeds
1/3 cup toasted pecans, chopped
1/3 cup of brown sugar
1/3 cup of pumpkin puree
¼ cup of applesauce
2 tablespoons of maple syrup
¾ teaspoon of pumpkin pie spice
½ teaspoon of cinnamon
¼ teaspoon of nutmeg
¼ teaspoon of salt
½ teaspoon of vanilla extract

Line a baking sheet with parchment paper. In a bowl mix oats, spices and salt. In a second bowl, combine brown sugar, pumpkin puree, applesauce, maple syrup and vanilla extract. Whisk until smooth. Pour wet ingredients into oat mixture and stir until oats are coated. Spread mixture on the baking sheet. Bake at 325 degrees for 20 minutes. Stir granola. Bake for an additional 20 minutes or until the granola is crisp and golden. Add pumpkin seeds and pecans to the sheet in the last 4 minutes of baking. After removing from oven add dried cranberries. Let cool.

RED PEPPER & TOMATO SOUP

2 cups of vegetable broth
1 cup of milk
30 ounces of crushed tomatoes, canned
12 ounce jar of roasted red peppers
1 yellow onion, diced
4 cloves of garlic, minced
2 tablespoons of all-purpose flour
2 tablespoons of butter
¼ tsp dried basil
Pinch of dried thyme
Freshly cracked Pepper

Mix onion, garlic and butter in a pot. Sauté over medium heat for 5 minutes or until onions are soft and transparent. Add flour, stir and cook for 2 minutes. The flour forms a paste with the butter and onions. When the flour paste turns slightly golden, remove it from the heat. Put crushed tomatoes with juices, roasted red peppers (without juices) and the flour paste into a food processor or blender. Blend until smooth, then return contents to the pot. Add vegetable broth, basil, thyme, and freshly cracked pepper and stir to combine. Heat and stir over a medium flame until soup begins to simmer. Turn off the heat. Add the milk and stir to combine.

RED WINE MARINATED STEAK

Steak of choice, tenderized
4 tablespoons of red wine
2 tablespoons of olive oil
1 tablespoon of soy sauce
1 tablespoon of apple cider vinegar
1 tablespoon of honey
1 tablespoon of Dijon mustard

Thoroughly combine the red wine, soy sauce, apple cider vinegar, honey, Dijon mustard and olive oil to create the marinade. Put the steak in a Ziploc bag with the marinade, removing as much of the air as possible. Place the steak in the refrigerator for 2 to 12 hours, depending on how much flavor you want to impart on the meat. To cook, use a skillet or cast iron skillet. Pour a little oil in the pan and heat to medium high. Sear the steak in the oil until it reaches desired doneness.

ROOT BEER BARBECUE SAUCE

1 cup of root beer
1 cup of ketchup
¼ cup of Worcestershire sauce
¼ cup of light brown sugar, packed
1 tablespoon of olive oil
1 tablespoon of garlic, minced
¼ teaspoon of salt
Pinch of pepper

In a pot sauté garlic in olive oil over medium low heat for 2 minutes or until it browns. Stir in root beer, ketchup, Worcestershire sauce and brown sugar. Mix thoroughly and bring to a boil. Reduce to a simmer for 7 minutes and stir occasionally. Remove from heat and stir in salt and pepper.

ROSEMARY & SESAME PECANS

1 pound of pecan halves
1 cup of raw sugar
¼ cup of sesame seeds
2 egg whites
1 tablespoon of kosher salt
1 tablespoon of rosemary, minced

In a bowl mix together sugar, salt, rosemary and sesame seeds. In a second bowl whisk the egg whites until a little frothy and stir in pecans until they are coated. Toss pecans with the dry mixture until evenly coated. Spread pecans on a lined cookie sheet. Bake at 300 degrees for 20 to 25 minutes until nuts are toasted and coating is dry.

RUSTIC GOURMET HERB JERKY

If possible, use fresh herbs when making this recipe.

3 pounds of lean beef, trimmed of fat
¼ cup of white wine vinegar
¼ cup of rosemary
¼ cup of parsley
3 tablespoons of oregano
2 tablespoons of sage
2 cloves of garlic, diced
2 tablespoons of kosher salt
2 tablespoons of pepper, fresh ground

Mix all of the ingredients, except the meat, in a blender or food processor. Slice beef against the grain and into ¼-inch strips or thinner. Coat each strip thoroughly with the mixture. Seal meat in a plastic bag or bowl with a lid and place in the refrigerator for 12 to 24 hours. You want to give the meat time to really absorb the flavors of the herbs. Place the meat on a baking rack on top of a cookie sheet. Bake at 160 degrees for 6 to 8 hours. Jerky should be dry, chewy and tender, not brittle or sharp. If needed, continue to bake until it reaches that point. If using a dehydrator, set on low between 150 to 160 degrees. Use only 1 tray. It could take 6 to 10 hours depending on the unit and the meat.

SALMON CHOWDER

2 pounds of salmon, canned or fresh
15 ounces of creamed corn
12 ounces of evaporated milk
8 ounces of cheddar cheese, shredded
2 cups of potatoes, diced
2 cups of chicken broth
2 carrots, diced
¾ cup of onion, diced
½ cup of celery, diced
3 tablespoons of butter
1 teaspoon of garlic powder
1 teaspoon of salt
1 teaspoon of pepper
1 teaspoon of dill

Melt butter in a large pot. Sauté onion, celery and garlic powder over medium heat until onions are tender. Stir in broth, potatoes, carrots, salt, pepper and dill. Bring to a boil and reduce heat. Cover and simmer for 20 minutes. Cut salmon into pieces or flakes. Add the salmon, evaporated milk, corn and cheese. Cook until thoroughly heated.

SESAME ALMOND NOODLES

8 ounces of spaghetti
3 tablespoons of soy sauce, low sodium
2 tablespoons of unsalted creamy almond
  butter
2 tablespoons of rice vinegar
1 tablespoon of sesame oil
Crushed red pepper flakes to taste

Cook spaghetti to al dente in a pot of salted water according to package directions. Drain and rinse with cold water to stop cooking and set aside. In a small bowl, combine almond butter, rice vinegar, soy sauce and sesame oil. Stir to combine thoroughly. Let rest for a few minutes to allow almond butter to dissolve. If sauce is too thick, add a little water to thin out. Once sauce is smooth, pour over cooked spaghetti noodles. Toss to combine. Sprinkle with crushed red pepper flakes to taste and toss again.

STEAK ON A STICK

2 pounds of sirloin steak
1 cup of soy sauce
½ cup of vegetable oil
¼ cup of molasses
4 cloves of garlic, minced
2 teaspoon of dry mustard
2 teaspoons of fresh ginger

Soak bamboo skewers in water so they won't burn during cooking. Slice meat against the grain into long strips and set aside. Combine remaining ingredients and mix thoroughly to create a marinade. Combine the meat and the liquid in a Ziploc bag and marinate in the refrigerator for 1 hour or more. Remove the meat from the refrigerator and thread the steak onto the skewers. Broil or grill the skewers until they reach desired doneness.

SUNFLOWER HUMMUS

28 ounces of garbanzo beans
¼ cup of olive juice
4 cloves of garlic, minced fine
1 cup of sunflower seeds
1 tablespoon of olive oil
1 teaspoon of salt

Drain and rinse the garbanzo beans thoroughly. Put the sunflower seeds in a food processor and process into a meal. Add beans, garlic, olive oil and salt to the seeds and process again. Add small amounts of olive juice (or water) and process until it reaches desired consistency.

SWEET POTATO WEDGES

2 large sweet potatoes cut into wedges
   (peeled or unpeeled is your choice)
2½ tablespoons of olive oil
1tablespoon of Italian seasoning
1½ teaspoons of sea salt
1 teaspoon of sugar
½ teaspoon of pepper

Cut off the pointy ends of the sweet potato wedges. Place the wedges in a large bowl and toss with olive oil, salt, sugar, seasoning and pepper. Mix well making sure each wedge is well coated. Put a piece of aluminum foil shiny side up on a baking sheet. Put the wedges on the sheet and bake at 450 degrees for 30 minutes. To make them crisper, place the wedges under a broiler for 3 to 5 minutes. Don't let them burn.

TATER TOT SKEWERS

1 bag of tater tots
8 slices of bacon, cooked and chopped
1 cup of cheddar cheese, grated fine
1 tablespoon of ranch seasoning
Wooden skewers

Cook tater tots according to directions on the bag. 400 degrees for 25 to 30 minutes usually works. After cooking, let them cool for 3 to 4 minutes and thread 6 tots per skewer. Lay the skewers on a baking sheet. Sprinkle with ranch seasoning, bacon and cheese. Bake the skewers in the oven at 400 degrees for 8 to 10 minutes or until cheese is melted and golden. For a different taste, substitute bacon for ham or pulled pork and replace ranch seasoning with barbecue sauce.

TOFU BREAKFAST SCRAMBLE

7 ounces of tofu, well drained
1 scallion, diced fine
1 clove of garlic, minced
1 tablespoon of water
1 teaspoon of nutritional yeast
¼ teaspoon of turmeric
¼ teaspoon of cumin
¼ teaspoon of paprika
Pinch of salt
Black pepper to taste
Olive oil

In a bowl mix yeast, turmeric, cumin, paprika, salt, pepper and water. Put a small amount of olive oil in a skillet or use a spray. Once it reaches medium heat, add scallion and garlic and sauté for 2 minutes. Crumble tofu into the pan, sprinkle spice mixture over tofu evenly. Cook for 2 to 3 minutes or until tofu is completely heated.

VANILLA COFFEE FLOAT

1½ cups of cold brew coffee
    (recipe on page 25)
1 large scoop of French vanilla ice cream
Whip cream
Cocoa powder

Pour coffee into a tall glass. Add a scoop of French vanilla ice cream. Top with whipped cream and sprinkle with cocoa powder. For added flavor, stir in vanilla creamer or Bailey's Irish cream to the coffee.

VEGAN CHEESE

13½ ounces of full-fat coconut milk
1 tablespoon of potato starch powder
½ tablespoon of tapioca flour or starch
5 tablespoons of water
1 tablespoon of coconut oil
3 teaspoons of agar powder
1½ teaspoons of coconut vinegar
1 teaspoon of salt
1 teaspoon of xantham gum

Mix potato starch and tapioca flour with the water in a bowl and stir until dissolved. Heat coconut milk in a saucepan over medium heat until it comes to a low boil. Place the coconut oil and xantham gum in a mixer on its highest setting and blend for a few seconds. Once the coconut milk has achieved a low boil, add the agar powder and whisk until dissolved, then add vinegar and salt. Reduce the stovetop heat to its lowest setting, and add in the flour mixture and the xantham gum/oil mixture, whisking quickly to combine. Transfer to a small-cubed silicone ice cube tray before it gets too thick to pour. Place in the refrigerator for a few hours to fully set. You now have vegan mozzarella.

VEGAN CHILI

30 ounces of canned red kidney beans
14 ounces of tomatoes, canned and diced
  (You can use fresh tomatoes too)
½ cup of dried lentils
1 tablespoon of olive oil
1 onion, chopped and peeled
1 red pepper chopped with no seeds
1½ cloves of garlic crushed
1 teaspoon of paprika
2 tablespoons of chili powder
Salt and black pepper
¼ teaspoon of sugar

Simmer lentils and beans in water for 40 to 45 minutes, until tender. Heat oil in a large pan and sauté onion and pepper for 10 minutes. Add in garlic and cook for 1 to 2 minutes and then add tomatoes. Drain the beans and lentils, reserving the liquid. Add beans and lentils to the tomato mixture with the chili powder and paprika. Simmer for 15 minutes, pouring in the bean water as needed for consistency. Season and add sugar.

VEGAN COLESLAW

1 head of green cabbage, sliced thin
3 carrots, grated
1/3 cup of egg-free mayonnaise (vegan)
3 tablespoons of white vinegar
2 tablespoons of soy milk
1 tablespoon of sugar

Whisk together the mayonnaise, vinegar, sugar, soy milk, salt and pepper until smooth and creamy to make a dressing. In a bowl, combine cabbage and the grated carrots, and add the mayonnaise and vinegar dressing. Toss it together to combine well and to make sure that the all of the cabbage and carrots are evenly coated with the dressing. Chill for at least 2 hours in the refrigerator.

VEGAN MOLASSES COOKIES

½ tablespoon of ground flax mixed with
   2 tablespoons of water
¼ cup of vegan butter
¼ cup of natural cane sugar
2 tablespoons of blackstrap molasses
2 tablespoons of pure 100% maple syrup
½ teaspoon of pure vanilla extract
1 teaspoon of ground ginger
½ teaspoon of ground cinnamon
½ teaspoon of baking soda
¼ teaspoon of fine sea salt
¼ teaspoon of ground cloves
1¼ cups of light spelt flour
3 tablespoons sugar, for rolling

Mix flax and water and set aside. Stir to combine. In a bowl, thoroughly combine butter, cane sugar, molasses, maple syrup, vanilla, and flax/water mixture until smooth. In the same bowl, stir in one-by-one, ginger, cinnamon, soda, salt, cloves, and flour until just combined. Do not over mix. Form dough into small balls and roll in a bowl of sugar. Place balls on a parchment lined cookie sheet. Flatten balls slightly so they're ½-inch thick. Bake cookies at 350 degrees for 10 minutes for a soft cookie, 12 minutes for a crisp cookie.

VIOLET & MANGO SALAD

¼ cup of violet leaves (NOT African violet)
8 violets, stemmed, rinsed and patted dry
1 mango, peeled and diced large
   (or fruit of choice)
1 teaspoon of olive oil
1 teaspoon of balsamic vinegar
1 teaspoon of thyme
1 teaspoon of honey
Salt and pepper to taste

Mix oil, vinegar, honey, thyme, salt and pepper together to make the dressing. Toss violet leaves and mango with the dressing. When serving the salad, sprinkle violet petals on top.

WAFFLE BURGER

6 slices of whole-wheat bread
½ pound of ground beef, cooked
½ cup of onion, diced
3 tablespoons of ketchup
½ cup of corn, drained
2 teaspoons of salt
1 teaspoon of sugar
Butter
Pinch of pepper

Mix ground beef, onion, ketchup, salt, sugar, corn and pepper together. Spread mixture on one slice of bread and cover with a second slice. Butter the outside of the 2 slices and place in a heated waffle iron and bake for 2 to 3 minutes. You can also make this with a Panini press or sandwich maker.

WASABI SLIDERS

1½ pounds of ground beef
2 tablespoons of Kikkoman's Wasabi Sauce
½ cup of barbecue sauce
1 teaspoon of onion powder
Cheddar cheese, sliced
Dinner rolls
Miracle Whip (optional)

Mix ground beef with Wasabi Sauce, barbecue sauce, and onion powder. Pre-heat skillet, and shape ground beef into small slider patties. When patties are cooked through, add Cheddar cheese and melt. Warm the dinner rolls until slightly crisp on top. Spread Miracle Whip (optional) on each roll and add patty. If you want to turn up the heat, add a little extra Wasabi sauce to the mixture.

WEDGE SALAD ON A STICK

1 head iceberg lettuce
8 slices of bacon, cooked
1 avocado, diced
4 tomatoes, quartered
  (or 16 cherry tomatoes)
½ red onion, diced fine
¼ cup of blue cheese crumbles
½ cup of salad dressing
Fresh pepper to taste
16 wooden skewers

Remove wilted outer layers of lettuce and the stem. Slice the head of lettuce into quarters, then slice lettuce into "bite sized" chunks. To assemble skewers, layer lettuce, ½ slice bacon, avocado chunk, and tomato wedge (or cherry tomato). Drizzle dressing on skewers, and top with red onion and bleu cheese crumbles; add freshly ground pepper to taste.

WILD SALMON BROWN RICE CASSEROLE

16 ounces of canned or fresh wild salmon
1 cup of whole grain brown rice
1½ cups of frozen peas
¾ cup of 2% milk
2 tablespoons of butter
2 tablespoons of whole-wheat flour
1 tablespoon of onion powder
1 teaspoon of celery seed
Water

If using canned salmon, open and drain. Mash and remove any bones. Set aside. Melt butter in a pan. Stir in flour and cook to make a white sauce. Stir in milk, celery seed and onion powder. Cook while stirring slowly until it starts to thicken. Remove from the heat. Prepare rice according to package directions using just water. In another pan bring 1 cup of water to boil, add frozen peas to the water, cover and remove from heat. When rice is finished, mix rice with salmon, white sauce, and peas. Put the mixture in a casserole dish and cover with a lid or foil. Heat at 350 degrees for 25 minutes.

YOGURT COVERED BLUEBERRY KABOBS

Yogurt
Blueberries, fresh and washed
Wooden Skewers

Slide the blueberries onto the skewers. Pour the yogurt into a shallow bowl. Lay the kabobs in the yogurt and roll until fully and evenly covered. Place skewers in a jar and store in the freezer until they set up.

If you liked this book you may like Tim Murphy's other titles including his "cookbooks for guys" series including:

THE ROCK & ROLL COOKBOOK
"You Cook Me All Night Long"

THE SINGLE GUY COOKBOOK
"Simple Recipes Using 6 Ingredients or Less"

THE SECRET AGENT COOKBOOK
"A Dossier of Classified Recipes"

A TASTE OF THE 80's COOKBOOK
"The Joystick of Cooking"

FLANNEL JOHN'S FISHING & HUNTING CAMP COOKBOOK
"A Good Meal Makes for a Good Day"

FLANNEL JOHN'S MAN CANDY COOKBOOK
"Bacon, Bacon and More Bacon"

For more information on all 60 of his titles visit www.flanneljohn.com.